9/14

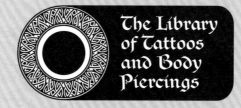
The Library
of Tattoos
and Body
Piercings

Tattoos,
Body Piercings,
and Teens

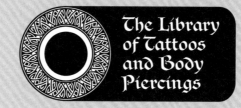

The Library
of Tattoos
and Body
Piercings

Tattoos,
Body Piercings,
and Teens

Other titles in the Library of Tattoos and Body Piercings series:

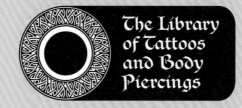

The Library
of Tattoos
and Body
Piercings

Tattoos, Body Piercings, and Teens

By Leanne Currie-McGhee

ReferencePoint Press®

San Diego, CA

ReferencePoint Press®

© 2014 ReferencePoint Press, Inc.
Printed in the United States

For more information, contact:
ReferencePoint Press, Inc.
PO Box 27779
San Diego, CA 92198
www.ReferencePointPress.com

LIBRARY OF CONGRESS CATALOGING-IN-PUBLICATION DATA

Currie-McGhee, L. K. (Leanne K.)
  Tattoos, body piercings, and teens / by Leanne Currie-McGhee.
     pages cm. -- (The library of tattoos and body piercings series)
  Includes bibliographical references and index.
  ISBN-13: 978-1-60152-566-6 (hardback)
  ISBN-10: 1-60152-566-4 (hardback)
  1. Tattooing. 2. Body piercing. 3. Teenagers--Social conditions. I. Title.
  GT2345.C87 2014
  391.6'50835--dc23
                                                                2012049320

Contents

More than a Trend

Harry Styles, a member of the popular band One Direction, decided to show something new to his fans in the fall of 2012. On Twitter, eighteen-year-old Styles revealed his latest inking, a tattoo of two swallows flying on his chest. Magazines reported that Styles sat for five hours as the tattoo was completed, but he did not mind the wait, as he was pleased with the result. "I like [this] kind of style of [tattoo], like the old sailor kind of tattoos. They symbolize traveling, and we travel a lot!"[1] Styles said. This tattoo is just one of many of Styles's growing collection of shoulder, chest, arm, and wrist tattoos. Styles is not alone in his love of tattoos. His bandmates also sport tattoos, as do several others of today's young celebrities.

Tattoos are not the only body art embraced by teen stars. Famous young celebrities like Lucy Hale, Lindsay Lohan, and Kesha have pierced body parts such as their tongues, belly buttons, lips, and noses. Many of these celebrities use their piercings as a way to express their individual fashion sense and unique styles.

Often young celebrities do not stop with just one tattoo or piercing. After the first tattoo or piercing they quickly move on to the next. For example, Kendall Schmidt of the television show *Big Time Rush* has four tattoos, and pop singer and Grammy winner Rihanna has multiple piercings and tattoos.

Everyday Teens

The tattooing and piercing trends among young celebrities have led to a rising number of pierced and tattooed teenagers. Just a few decades ago, seeing a teen with a tattoo or piercing was uncommon. Today, coming across a teen who is tattooed, pierced, or even both is not unusual. An Italian 2010 study included in the US National Library of Medicine found that 4 percent of Italian adolescents sported tattoos, 24 percent had piercings, and 2.5 percent had both.

Today, an increasing number of teens are turning to tattoos and piercings as a way to decorate their bodies, express their personalities, and assert their individuality. For Sparrow, an art student, getting a tattoo was a way to remember her youth. At nineteen years old she designed a tattoo of a bird and had it tattooed on her neck. "I'm

Pop singer Rihanna has multiple piercings and tattoos, including a strand of stars cascading down her neck (pictured). The growing teen affinity for tattoos and body piercings has been influenced, at least in part, by young celebrities such as Rihanna.

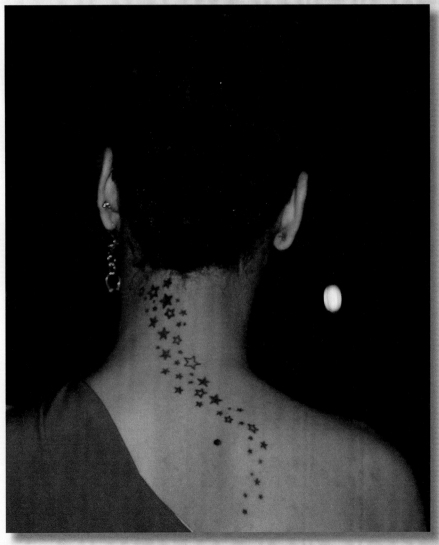

going to remember what it was like being 19 years old in art school and I love that . . . you shouldn't be afraid to get a tattoo you really like as long as it has a lot of meaning behind it,"[2] Sparrow says of her tattoo.

Addiction?

Although Sparrow was satisfied with just one tattoo, many teens find themselves, like celebrities, moving on to multiple tattoos or piercings after their first one. In fact, many teens choose to continue getting pierced or tattooed on a regular basis. Although studies have not significantly linked tattoos to addiction, people who go back again and again talk about feeling addicted. But what are they addicted to?

The experience of getting a tattoo is one possibility. In response to physical threat, excitement, or pain the body releases adrenaline. The body also releases endorphins, which are natural pain relievers. The process of tattooing can be painful but adrenaline and endorphins can create a sense of pleasure or well-being—feelings the person wants to experience again and again.

Another possibility is that people become addicted to the attention that they receive from their tattoos or piercings. A person with a visible tattoo or piercing is likely to receive comments from others about their body art. For people who crave attention, these comments, whether positive or negative, could lead them to get more tattoos and piercings in order to generate more attention.

Still another reason people become compulsive about body piercings and tattoos is that they may be collectors. Instead of choosing to collect physical items, some people choose to collect body art. They see their body as a canvas on which they can store and display their collection.

A Unique Look

Teens get multiple tattoos or piercings for many reasons, some of which might have nothing to do with addiction. Some teens just really like the way tattoos and piercings look. As a sophomore at Hastings High School in Nebraska, John Cook already has three tattoos, including a skull on his left shin, another skull on his left shoulder, and a trio of roses on his lower back. Cook is already planning his next tattoos.

Crystal Milam also has plans for the future body art. By the time she was a junior at North Hardin High School in Radcliff, Kentucky, she had six piercings on her right ear and three on her left ear. She plans to get more in the future. "I really like how my piercings on my ears look," Milam says. "I think by having a lot it makes me different than everyone else."[3]

Whether an addiction or not, today's teens, both celebrities and non-celebrities, are embracing tattoos and body piercings. Because these types of body art are long-term, the decision to get tattooed or pierced is a serious one that comes with health, societal, and emotional implications. Teens need to examine the implications before making body art decisions.

Chapter One

Adorning Their Bodies

Kimberly O'Connor always knew she was different from everybody else. As a teen, she decided that body art was the perfect tool to display her uniqueness. For her first body art choice, she stretched her earlobes via piercing and, soon after, she walked into a tattoo shop in Blooming-ton, California. She thought carefully about what she wanted the tattoo to look like and what it would mean for her. "My first tattoo is on my shoulder, a heart rocket with the moon. It represents that when I meet the right guy, he'll have the key to my heart,"[4] O'Connor says.

Since then O'Connor's love of body art has grown, and she has con-tinued to get tattooed by the same tattoo artist. It has taken over one hundred cumulative hours to cover her arms and legs with tattoos. To her, each tattoo is meaningful and represents something important in her life. Although it has been several years since she got her first tattoo and stretched her earlobes, she does not regret either decision. She considers her body art an outer reflection of her inner self and sees herself continu-ing to decorate her body, as a way to show her emotional growth, for years to come.

How Popular Is Body Art?

Body piercing and tattoos have grown in popularity among teens and young adults. Statistics show that such body art is much more main-stream today than it was in the past. For example, a 2010 study by the Children's Hospital of Philadelphia found that up to 35 percent of American youth aged eleven to twenty-five has some form of body art.

Permanent body art's popularity has soared in the past two decades, and statistics show that teens and young adults in particular have embraced this trend. Harris Interactive conducted an online poll in 2012 to determine what percentage of people had tattoos, their ages, and overall thoughts about how tattoos make them feel. The poll revealed that 22 percent of survey participants between 18 and 24 years old had a tattoo, up 13 percent from a Harris 2008 poll on the same topic. Pew Research Center conducted a similar poll on the popularity of tattoos among different age groups in 2010. Pew's poll found that tattoos are more popular among young adults (38 percent of people aged 18 to 29 have at least one tattoo) than among the population overall (28 percent of the general population has at least one tattoo). The survey also found that males and females between the ages of 18 and 29 were nearly equally likely to have tattoos. "I think that among the younger generations, tattooing is becoming more acceptable,"[5] says Emily Bosch, a college student who got her first tattoo as a sophomore.

As with tattoos, studies show that piercing is most popular among younger generations. Additionally, piercing is more popular with females than males. The Pew Research Center found that nearly one in four Americans between the ages of 18 and 29 has a piercing in some place other than an earlobe, which is about six times more than older adults. According to Glenn Braunstein, chairman of the Department of Medicine, Cedars-Sinai, research shows that as many as 56 percent of teens and young adults aged 17 to 25 are pierced. According to Pew, 35 percent of women in the 18 to 29 age group have a piercing other than in the earlobe compared to 11 percent of the males. Braunstein writes of the popularity of piercings among youth, stating, "Piercings from head to toe—and pretty much anywhere in between—have gone mainstream."[6]

Many young adults and teens find that they want both piercings and tattoos. A survey published in 2008 by a team of professors at Texas State University concluded that approximately 16 percent of persons aged eighteen to twenty-four have both piercings and tattoos. Another study by the Harris Poll found that among those with tattoos, as many as 16 percent also had a piercing on their body, compared to just 3 percent of those with no tattoo. For many, getting a tattoo or piercing seems to make it easier to continue to try new body art and leads to more adornments.

Today's Trends

Several trends have accompanied the popularity of tattoos and piercings. One current tattoo trend among teens is to get multiple tattoos. For example, by the time Shannon Carter was a senior in high school she had several tattoos. One of them was a tattoo on her wrist that stated "All Love, No Lies" and another was a koi fish on her side. She explained that getting tattoos can be addictive and once she got one, she wanted more. A 2010 Pew Research Center study found that about half of the tattooed people aged 18 to 29 have two to five tattoos and 18 percent have six or more.

Other trends include getting large tattoos and placing them in visible locations on the body as opposed to the small, discreet tattoos that used to be more common. Full sleeve tattoos, which are particularly popular among young men, cover a large portion of a person's arm. Teens are also choosing to place large tattoos on their backs. Additionally, teens are opting to get tattoos in places that cannot be covered, such as on the hands and lower arms. Vince Hemingson, creator of The Vanishing Tattoo, one of the Internet's largest, most popular, and critically acclaimed websites related to tattoos and body art, has followed trends over the years. He has found that lower back and foot and ankle tattoos are popular among women. Men, according to Hemingson, tend toward upper arm tattoos and chest tattoos. Rising in popularity are tattoos on the wrists and hands, particularly among male and female teens, and the rib cage among young women.

Among the most popular tattoo designs today are script and lettering tattoos, says Rocky Rakovic, editor of *Inked* magazine. Rakovic also has found that the trend of tribal tattoos, tattoos that originated with tribal warriors and are entirely done in black ink with bold, curved lines, is declining whereas realistic portrait tattoos, tattoos of specific people, are on the rise. Other tattoo artists say that butterflies and flowers continue to be the most requested tattoos by young women.

New trends have also developed with piercing. Where once the earlobe was the primary spot for piercing, now many teens sport rings or jewels on the tongue, navel, or nose, or even on their lips, eyelids, or

Earlobe stretching and multiple piercings are no longer a cultural oddity in the United States. One recent study found that up to 35 percent of US teens and young adults have some sort of body piercing or tattoo.

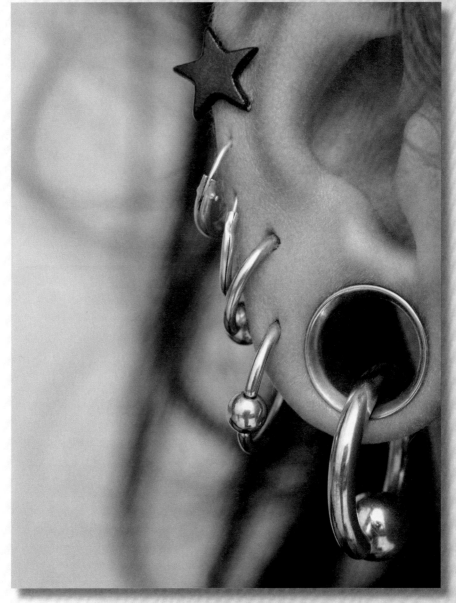

cheeks. As with tattoos, teens are also getting multiple piercings instead of just one or two.

With piercings, certain locations are more popular than others. According to Statistics Brain, aside from the earlobes the most popular piercing for women is the navel, then the nose, with the ear (other than earlobe) coming in third. Males prefer to pierce, in order of popularity, their nipples, eyebrows, and parts of their ears.

Cultural Influences

Tattoos and body piercings have become popular among teens for many reasons, and one of these is the influence of pop culture. Television, especially reality TV, has embraced body art. Several cable channels feature shows that center on the tattoo industry.

Over the past decade numerous reality television shows about tattoo artists and their work have sprung up on different channels. The cable channel TLC has aired several tattoo-related reality shows and continues to renew them due to their popularity. The latest one, which premiered in the spring of 2012, is *Tattoo School*, which follows people who are attending a tattoo-training course. Other shows on TLC have included *LA Ink*, *Miami Ink*, and *NYC Ink*, all of which followed the

Tattoo Togetherness

Not only are parents today more receptive to tattoos than they were a decade ago, some are even joining their kids in getting a tattoo. This is true among everyday people as well as celebrities. For example, when pop star Justin Bieber was seventeen he and his father had the word *Yeshua*, the Hebrew word for "Jesus," tattooed vertically on their left torsos. Bieber chose this tattoo because of the importance of his faith, and he did it with his father because, although raised mainly by his mother, Bieber has remained close to his father. His father, already sporting many tattoos, chose to get the tattoo as a way to bond with his son and show his faith.

lives of people running tattoo shops, how they do their work, and what the finished tattoos look like. *LA Ink* had the highest-rated series premiere in the history of TLC among adults aged eighteen to thirty-four. *Ink Master*, a reality show on Spike TV that follows tattoo artists as they compete against each other for a $100,000 prize, was the highest-rated original series for Spike TV in 2012 with an average of 1.8 million weekly viewers.

Some tattoo artists have linked the rise in teenage clients to these television shows. Tim Lund, a tattoo artist in North Dakota, has seen a major increase in teen and young adults as customers over the past decade. The rising number of young clients, he says, "has a lot to do with television shows. Ten or fifteen years ago, you hardly could see tattoos on people, and now they're all over."[7]

Celebrity Influence

Celebrities are another major influence on teens, who often follow the trends and fashions of their favorites. Many celebrities, including those in their teens, get their bodies pierced and tattooed for all to see. When these celebrities publicly display their body art, it encourages those who idolize them to do the same. "Many teen celebrities do have real tattoos," writes Stacey Goldmeier, vice president of Atlantic Laser Tattoo Removal. "But not only do they have tattoos, they love to show them off. Of course, the media loves to show and point out celebrity tattoos as well."[8]

Teen celebrities often adorn themselves with not just one, but two or more piercings and/or tattoos. Singer/actress Miley Cyrus first pierced her nose at age seventeen in 2009. Cyrus also is decorated with multiple tattoos, many of which she got before turning eighteen. Singer Justin Bieber also sports several tattoos, his latest an inking of Jesus on his leg. In 2012 famous tattoo artist Bang Bang tattooed actress Selena Gomez's neck with the Roman numerals for 76 as a tribute to a family member important to her, reports E! Online. Prior to this tattoo, Gomez got a small heart tattooed on her right wrist.

Aside from pop stars and actresses, famous athletes with tattoos and piercings also influence teens today. During the 2012 Olympics many of the athletes from all countries showed off their tattoos in magazines and on television. The Olympic rings were a popular tattoo among athletes, including US gymnast Jonathan Horton, German swimmer Sarah Poewe, and US swimmer Ryan Lochte. Aside from Olympians, professional sports figures from basketball to football also sport tattoos. Their tattoos often can be seen both on and off the fields. For example, basketball player Gilbert Arenas of the Washington Wizards created a tribute to President Barack Obama with a tattoo of the words "change we believe in" on each finger of his left hand.

The Reasons Why

Although cultural influences make teens aware of body art and may increase their interest in it, their reasons for actually making the decision to get pierced or tattooed are varied. Some are well thought out, with the body art being meaningful, while others are impulsive, spur-of-the-moment decisions.

Many of these teens get tattoos or piercings that they believe are beautiful and interesting and enhance how they look and feel. One such person is Danielle Loftus, age twenty-two, who lives in Philadelphia, works at a local preschool, and is pierced and tattooed. She got her first piercing on her navel when she was sixteen years old and at eighteen decided to have a star with wings tattooed on her lower back. She likes tattoos because "I'm intrigued by them. It's interesting to have stuff you want on yourself forever. They show style, personality. I don't like plain, boring."[9]

Other teens decide to get pierced or tattooed as a way to commemorate an important event in their lives. In 2012 a thirteen-year-old boy named Andrew explained on KIRO 7, a Seattle, Washington, news show, that he decided to get a six-inch dragon tattooed on his chest to signify his victory

Large, elaborate tattoos are gaining in popularity. Some cover the length of an arm or leg while others, such as this detailed and brightly colored koi fish, use the entire back as a canvas.

over leukemia. He obtained the tattoo illegally, without his parents' permission, although prior to that he and his mother both had gone together to get tattoos on their ankles to commemorate another medical emergency that he had overcome. Although his parents are unhappy with his actions, Andrew does not regret getting a tattoo. "This is my badge of honor," says Andrew as he displays his tattoo. "Strength and courage and warrior."[10]

Some teens choose to honor a person special to them by getting a tattoo depicting the person or something that symbolizes that person. Nick Sloan decided to get a tattoo at age seventeen to honor the memory of his grandfather. His parents were supportive and signed a consent for him, since he was a minor and the state of Delaware requires written consent for minors to get a tattoo. "I picked a funny old German cartoon, and [my parents] agreed that was a great way to remember him,"[11] Sloan recalls.

Different Decisions

Although many teens have meaningful reasons for getting body art, others simply do it as a way to rebel. Some choose to get body art because it is a way to be different from others in their school or social circle. In a 2012 Harris Poll, about one-fourth of tattoo-bearing young people polled agreed that it made them feel more rebellious.

Still other teens choose to get a tattoo or piercing as a spur-of-the-moment decision. At times this is because the teen has been partying and is inebriated, and making an informed decision is less likely. Although some tattoo artists and piercers will not work on someone who is obviously intoxicated, others will.

At other times a teen may get pierced or tattooed because of pressure from friends. In 2012 Eunice On-yelobi was a senior at Kenwood Academy High in Illinois and already had fourteen tattoos. She attributes her first tattoo to pressure from her friends. "A big reason why I wanted to get tattoos was indeed peer pressure," she said. "And once I got my first one, I got addicted."[12]

Parent Involvement

Another reason more teens may be getting body art is that parent approval is easier to get today

Piercing as a Reward for Good Grades

Some US teens receive rewards from their parents for good grades. Often the reward is cash, but fifteen-year-old Kyler Shonhart asked for his reward to be two piercings under his lower lip. In July 2012 Kyler got his wish. "I got the snake bites (two piercings just under the bottom lip) because Skrillex (a musician) has them and I kind of thought it would be fun to look like him even more," Kyler says. Kyler's mother, Rachel, encourages her children to show their individuality and had no problem with Kyler's choice. "If I allow him to be who he wants to be, I think that prevents a bigger rebellion later and they are more secure in who they are," she says. For now, Kyler says he is not interested in more piercings and is happy with his snake bite.

Quoted in Danielle Tyler, "Pittsfield Woman Starts Petition Regarding Piercing Rule," *Pike County Express*, October 3, 2012. http://pikecountyexpress.com.

than in the past, and this makes it easier to get required consent for legal tattoos and piercings. A recent poll by Café Mom, a national online community of mothers, found that 15 percent of moms polled said they would allow their teen get a tattoo, while 30 percent were either uncertain or open to the idea, depending on the circumstances. Kathy Linthicum of Arkansas accompanied her son, Matthew Weiss, to a tattoo parlor to give him his birthday present—a tattoo of a cross. He had been asking for it for several months, and she had been reluctant to allow him to get a tattoo but eventually relented.

Other parents, however, are reluctant to allow their children to get body art at a young age because it is permanent and has long-lasting implications. Some teens choose to get tattoos or piercings in secret to avoid dealing with their parents. Amy Kaufman waited until she was eighteen to get a tattoo, so she did not need her parents' permission to legally get a tattoo. She opted for a star on her lower back and kept the secret from her parents for months because she was afraid of their reaction. However, when she finally told them, their reaction was not what she expected. "Showing my parents the tattoo was anticlimactic. . . . More than anything, they were relieved that it was small and tasteful,"[13] Kaufman recalls.

Whether parents are approving or not, teens continue to get pierced and tattooed. The popularity of both piercings and tattoos has steadily risen among teens and is continuing to increase. Their reasons vary, but ultimately many teens are deciding to decorate their bodies with permanent body art.

Chapter Two

Body Art Risks

Tattoos and body piercings come with risks. Both can result in health problems from minor to severe. To minimize the risks, owners of tattoo and body piercing studios in most states are required by law to register their businesses with the government, follow local health codes, and submit to health inspections. Body art practitioners in most states are required to complete a course that teaches how blood-borne pathogens are spread, how to avoid exposure, and what to do if exposed to infectious material. These practices are intended to keep customers safe, and most of the time they do—but not always.

Serious Health Risks

Both piercing and tattoo procedures make a person vulnerable to diseases transmitted by blood. The tattoo procedure typically includes using a handheld machine with a needle attached and piercing the skin repeatedly while inserting ink into the punctured skin. With a piercing, a person's skin is simply punctured with a needle. In both cases, if the needle has not been properly sterilized and has previously been used on a person with a virus, that person's virus may be on the needle and transmitted to the next person who undergoes the procedure.

The most serious health risk for people getting piercings or tattoos is infection with a blood-borne disease such as hepatitis B or hepatitis C. The Centers

Did You Know?

According to a 2012 study in the journal *Pediatric Dentistry*, more than three thousand people each year visit emergency rooms with oral injuries, such as an infection of the tongue, that are related to their mouth piercings.

for Disease Control (CDC) warns that both body piercing and tattoos can potentially cause either disease, particularly if a person goes to an unlicensed practitioner who may not follow health codes. Additionally, according to D. Jane Buxton of the British Columbia Centre for Disease Control in Vancouver, a 2010 review of 124 published studies from thirty countries shows that people with tattoos are three times as likely to have hepatitis C as those without tattoos.

Both diseases can lead to major health problems. Hepatitis B causes inflammation of the liver, which can impede proper function and sometimes lead to liver failure—a condition that requires a transplant. Hepatitis C can cause permanent scarring and impede liver function. In 2010 Michelle Silverthorne wrote an article that appeared in *Newsweek* magazine about how her life has been affected by hepatitis C. She believes she contracted the disease from a tattoo she got at age twenty-three. Since the diagnosis, she has dealt with many treatments and their side effects as well as the effects of the disease itself. "The side effects [of the drugs to treat hepatitis C] rendered the next 48 weeks an absolute hell. I lived with mood swings, irritability, irrational thoughts, and brain fog, along with rapid weight loss (the one really good side effect), unrelenting rashes on my hands and feet that made sleeping difficult, hypothyroidism, hair loss, and a host of other bizarre and equally annoying symptoms,"[14] Silverthorne wrote. Currently her disease is stable and she is continuing to manage it through treatment.

The liver is not the only organ that is at risk from poor tattoo and body piercing practices. Another serious health problem that can result from body art is endocarditis, an inflammation of the heart or valves. Untreated, this condition can result in heart failure. Endocarditis begins when certain types of germs enter the bloodstream, then travel to the heart. If a piercing or tattoo practitioner uses an unsterile needle, germs that cause endocarditis can enter the bloodstream of the person getting the body art. An article in the *Journal of the American Society of Echocardiography* reported in 2008 that a fifteen-year-old girl developed endo-

Did You Know?

A Northwestern University study of body piercing found that 31 percent of respondents with piercings developed health-related problems such as infections, scarring, and swelling.

carditis, which resulted in multiple large masses located on both right chambers of her heart, as a result of an infected navel piercing.

Less Serious, More Prevalent

Although serious health problems from piercings and tattoos are possible, less serious problems are more prevalent. Infections, allergic reactions, scarring, and other issues can occur from piercings and tattoos. Of these, infections are the most common.

Infections can occur when germs enter open wounds such as those made during piercing and tattoo procedures. Piercings, in particular, can

The typical tattoo artist uses a handheld device with a needle to pierce the skin and inject the ink. If the needle has not been properly sterilized it can transmit blood-borne infectious diseases.

lead to infections because piercings take longer to heal than tattoos. If proper aftercare procedures such as cleaning the wound are not followed during the healing time, infection is likely. A 2012 Northwestern University research survey showed that around 20 percent of all body piercings result in infections. Most of these are minor and localized. Typical symptoms associated with infections are pain, redness, swelling, and/or pus discharge. However, if not treated these infections can result in more serious problems, such as the infection spreading to other parts of the body, including the internal organs, and developing into problems such as endocarditis.

In 2012 health officials reported an outbreak of tattoo-related skin infections in Colorado, Iowa, New York, and Washington, with twenty-two confirmed cases and more than thirty suspected cases.

Suspended for Tattoo

Jessica Coffey claims she was not in a gang, but in 2010 she was suspended from her high school for having a gang-related tattoo. Coffey, then a senior at Riverdale High School in Fort Myers, Florida, was suspended from her school because of a tattoo on her left arm. The tattoo was not new; she had gotten it about two years earlier and apparently no one had noticed until one day when it came to the attention of a school administrator. Coffey said that the tattoo of two masks—one smiling and one crying—represented her twin sisters. But police say this image has also been associated with gangs. The assistant principal suspended her on the basis that the tattoo was gang-related. Coffey and her mother both insisted she was not in a gang and could not understand why she was suspended. However, the district's code of conduct states that students are not allowed to have gang-related tattoos, and it is up to school administrators to determine whether or not a tattoo is gang-related and how a student should be punished. As a result, Coffey had to attend an alternative high school during her ten-day suspension.

An investigation revealed that tattoo artists in those states had followed proper safety procedures but had unknowingly purchased unsterile ink for use in their work. "It's unfortunate that they can do everything right, but if the manufacturer doesn't supply them with sterile ink product it still results in them giving their clients infections,"[15] says CDC epidemiologist Tara MacCannell. The cause of the infections was a bacterial cousin of tuberculosis named *Mycobacterium chelonae*. The infections resulted in itchy and painful pus-filled blisters that took months to heal, and involved treatment with harsh antibiotics accompanied by unpleasant side effects.

Allergic reactions such as swelling, an itchy rash, or redness on the skin can result from tattoos and piercings. People may be allergic to certain metals used in piercing jewelry or inks used in tattoos. According to Mayo Clinic, red, green, yellow, and blue dyes more commonly cause allergic reactions than other colored inks, and these reactions can occur years after getting the tattoo. As for piercings, CNN reported that up to 15 percent of people are allergic to nickel, which is one type of metal used in piercing jewelry.

A variety of other common health issues can affect a person who gets tattooed or pierced. Both piercing and tattoos can leave scars after the wound from the piercing or tattoo heals. Piercings can result in body tears when jewelry catches on something like clothing. Also, jewelry from a tongue piercing often chips teeth when the tongue moves against them. Arthur Perry, a clinical surgeon, reports that nearly half of those with tongue piercings develop chipped teeth.

Increased Risk

The best way to avoid the risks associated with tattoos and body piercings is to choose a reputable practitioner. Some teens increase their chance of developing health problems because they get their body art from unlicensed practitioners. The reason they go to someone without a license is that many states have laws that require teens to get a parent's permission before getting pierced or tattooed. They can avoid these laws by getting pierced or tattooed illegally, but these illegal routes put them at greater risk of health complications.

Unlicensed tattoo artists or piercers might not know that that they need to sterilize every piece of equipment they use or have the necessary materials to sterilize all instruments properly. For these reasons, a teen who chooses to get body art from an unlicensed practitioner increases his or her risk of infection. Two teens in Newberg, Oregon, discovered the danger of getting tattoos from an unlicensed practitioner in 2012 when they decided to get tattooed by a fellow student. The two high school students who got the tattoos contracted MRSA, an infection caused by a staph bacteria that requires intense antibiotics to cure it. Misty Hines, the mother of one of the infected boys, took her son to the hospital a week after he got the tattoo because he became so ill. "I thought he had a collapsed lung, he also had a large open wound on the back of his right arm from where he got the tattoo,"[16] Hines recalls. Her son recovered, but without hospital intervention he could have become severely ill.

Societal Issues

Health risks are not the only issues associated with teen body art. Body art can negatively affect how a teen is perceived and treated by others, which can result in problems getting a job. While many employers are more accepting of body art than in the past, many others do not like their employees to show visible body art. Teens with tattoos and piercings may not get the job they desire because certain companies believe the tattoos and piercings are not professional looking.

Many teens and young adults discover that tattoos and body piercings are not totally accepted when they first apply for a job. This happened to Ariel Rivera when she came home from college for the summer and applied for a summer job. After an initial interview, Dorney Park & Wildwater Kingdom in Pennsylvania invited her back for a second interview for a job as a ride operator. Her excitement at being invited back was short-lived. At the interview, Rivera mentioned she had a tattoo on the

Did You Know?
A 2012 survey by Vault .com, a website that provides employment information about companies, found that 53 percent of respondents with tattoos cover them at work.

back of her neck and was immediately dismissed. "I felt discriminated against," said Rivera, a creative writing major at East Stroudsburg University. "I've never gotten in trouble. I don't drink. I don't do drugs—but I have a tattoo."[17]

Companies that deal directly with the public often have policies regarding visible body art that pierced and tattooed teens need to be aware of when applying for a job. For example, at Walt Disney World amusement park, body alterations like visible tattoos and body piercing are prohibited. At Chili's Bar and Grill restaurants, employees may not have facial piercings of any sort. Red Lobster's body modification rules state that employees who work in the front of the restaurant where they directly deal with customers cannot have visible tattoos or facial piercings. Teens with visible body art cannot work at these places.

The Military

Teens who get tattooed or pierced in high school may discover these choices negatively affect their lives after high school. Many teens want to enter the military after high school or go through college via the military branches' Reserve Officer Training Corps scholarships. Their body art may prohibit them from doing so depending on the extent and location of their piercings and tattoos.

Although the stereotypical image of a navy sailor includes a tattoo on his arm, today's navy and the other military branches have incorporated strict rules regarding body art. As body art has become more common and people are getting more visible tattoos and piercings, the military branches have responded by implementing policies that restrict how a military member can decorate himself or herself. The US Navy does not permit tattoos on the face, neck, or scalp; it also prohibits more extreme body modifications such as stretched ears. The air force does not allow excessive visible tattoos, which is defined as more than one-fourth of the visible body covered in tattoos, and, like the navy, this branch does not allow any piercings, outside of one pair of earlobe piercings for women. The army does not allow tattoos on the face, head, or neck. Additionally, neither men nor women may wear piercing jewelry while in army uniform, but women may wear earrings in pierced earlobes outside of

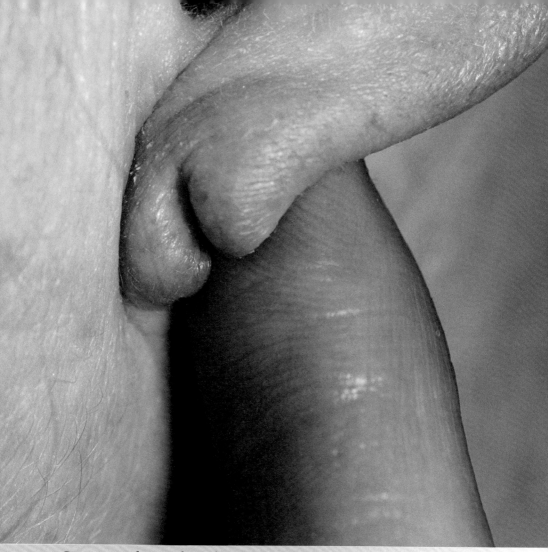

Recurrent infections from cheap, nonsterile metal earrings destroyed the tissue around the pierced earlobe and caused it to split. Infections and tears are among the risks that come with piercings and tattoos.

uniform. These are just some of the rules of the military branches, and they are strict about enforcing them.

Even if a teen has a tattoo that is on an accepted body part, such as the upper arm, a military branch may not allow a teen to join due to the words or pictures of the tattoo. In 2009 an eighteen-year-old from Tennessee enlisted in the marines but was rejected before he made it to boot camp. The reason is that he had a tattoo of a Confederate flag on his shoulder, which some people consider racist. If a tattoo can be perceived by anyone as racist, it is not allowed in the marines. Unfortunately for the teen, his dream of becoming a marine ended because of his tattoo choice.

School Issues

Being decorated with body art also has the potential to be a problem at school. Many high schools throughout the country limit and in some cases ban body art such as tattoos and piercings. For example, in Toronto, Canada, a Notre Dame Catholic High School ninth grade student, Mikaela Gunning-Pereira, was banned from her school because she wore a lip piercing. The Toronto District Catholic School Board allows nose piercings but not lip piercings. "It doesn't affect who she is as a person or as a student," says Mikaela's mother, Paula Gunning-Pereira. "It's bad

Beware of the Belly

Although all piercings risk infection, especially as they heal, a person who gets a navel piercing is particularly vulnerable to infection because the navel piercing takes the longest to heal of all the piercings. These piercings usually take six months to a year to heal properly. Erin Morris got a navel piercing after she turned eighteen. Although she went to a reputable piercer and followed aftercare instructions she still ended up with an infection. Her infection reached the point where she was prescribed antibiotics and warned that it could get worse. "The doctor also warned me how an infected belly button piercing like this could become very serious if not treated," Morris recalls. "So I had to keep a very close eye on the healing process; if it seemed like the infection wasn't going away, I was going to have to remove my piercing and undergo more aggressive treatment." Ultimately Morris did not have to remove the piercing, but it took several months, a doctor's visit, and antibiotics for her piercing to heal.

Erin Morris, "A Cure for Infected Belly Button Piercings," May 27, 2008, Yahoo News. http://voices.yahoo.com.

enough that kids bully other kids, but when individuals in a position of authority bully children it's unacceptable."[18]

High schools are not the only schools that impose rules about body art. Some colleges, typically religiously affiliated ones, also have rules regarding tattoos and piercings. Among them is Liberty University, a private Christian college in Virginia that does not allow body piercings by men or women, on or off campus. Similarly, at Brigham Young University, a Mormon affiliated school in Utah, women may wear one pair of earrings but no other piercing jewelry, and males cannot have any piercings.

Other schools that have implemented body art rules or negatively view body art are certain medical and nursing universities. For example, Missouri Southern State University nursing students may only have tattoos if they cannot be seen while the students are in uniform. Some medical schools also harbor negative attitudes toward people with visible body art. For this reason, medical school admissions consulting companies advise applicants not to wear body art during the in-person interviews that are part of the application process. "Do you really want to throw away your entire application on a piece of jewelry? If you want to make a statement, make sure you get into medical school first. Body piercings that show (nose ring, tongue ring, eyebrow ring, etc.) fall under the same general guidelines as earrings. Wear it if it is a huge part of who you are. Lose it for a day if it isn't,"[19] advises medical school admissions consultant Suzanne Miller, author of *The Medical School Admissions Guide: A Harvard MD's Week-by-Week Admissions Handbook*.

Did You Know?
The Norfolk, Virginia, police department bans tattoos that cover at least 30 percent of an exposed body part.

Friends and Family

Lastly, a decision to pierce or tattoo may adversely affect teens' relationships with their families and others they associate with on a daily basis. This is due to the fact that although piercings and tattoos are much more widely accepted than in the past, many still see tattoos and piercings in a negative light. According to a 2012 Harris Poll, half of those without a tattoo believe that someone with one is more rebellious.

For some parents, their child getting a tattoo or piercing, particularly without their permission, leads to anger and negativity in their relationship. Toi Jenkins told her fourteen-year-old son that he could not get a tattoo. She went out of town over Thanksgiving and returned to discover he had a tattoo on his left forearm. "That's something that's permanent on his body for the rest of his life," says Jenkins. "I'm angry at my son."[20]

Negative reactions from friends and others are just one of the many risks teens who decide to get pierced or tattooed may encounter. Health issues, school rules, and job implications are other potential areas of their lives that may be affected by their body art decisions. When teens make a decision to get inked or pierced, a thoughtful decision should take into consideration all of the potential implications, both positive and negative.

Chapter Three

Body Art, Teens, and the Law

Any teen who decides to get pierced or tattooed needs to be aware of body art laws. Although no federal law restricts minors from obtaining body art, several states have such restrictions. These laws either prohibit teens from getting body art or require teens to get consent from their parents before obtaining tattoos or piercings.

The body art laws that affect teens are determined by the state or city in which each teen lives. The laws are aimed at protecting them from making decisions with potential long-term implications, protecting body art professionals from being sued, and ensuring that parents are involved in the decision-making process.

Prohibited by Some

Tattooing minors is prohibited in certain parts of the United States. The most stringent of these prohibitions occur in states such as South Carolina, where a teen under age nineteen cannot legally get a tattoo, and in states such as New York and Minnesota, where the minimum age to legally obtain a tattoo is eighteen. A teen in Florida must wait until he or she is sixteen before getting a tattoo. A tattoo artist in any of these states who tattoos a minor is breaking the law and will face consequences. "You're committing a crime if you do this,"[21] says Peter Constantakes, New York Department of Health spokesman. The tattoo artist's punishment for this misdemeanor could include a fine and/or time in jail.

Certain states also prohibit piercing of minors, although in many cases the laws refer to specific types of piercings. A teen under eighteen in Minnesota may not legally get a nipple or genital piercing. In Idaho any teen under age fourteen may not legally get any piercing other than of the earlobes. Similarly, Wisconsin teens must be at least fifteen to get a body part pierced legally.

Many teens believe laws that forbid minors from getting body art are unfair because they think they are old enough to make their own decisions. "I don't think the law should tell us if we are too young for something that doesn't really hurt us," says Cassie Ruha, who legally got a tattoo at age sixteen in Minnesota before the law changed to prohibit teens under eighteen from getting tattoos. "It's just pictures on your skin."[22] Ruha believes that she and other teens are mature enough to understand the consequences of getting tattooed or pierced.

However, many parents and even professional piercers and tattoo artists believe that some type of oversight of minors is needed and that prohibiting younger teens from getting pierced or tattooed is the wise choice. "Anyone under 18 doesn't understand the commitment,"[23] says Brandon Heffron, who owns Beloved Studios, a tattoo studio in St. Paul, Minnesota. He wants teens to understand that body art is a major decision and the laws that prohibit certain types of body art for teens are in place to protect teens.

Consent First

Several states do allow teens to get piercings or tattoos as long as they have signed consent from a parent or legal guardian. This means that minors need to prove that their parents or legal guardians have given them approval to get a piercing or tattoo before body art practitioners will work on them. Consent laws are meant to protect minors from making long-term decisions that could adversely affect them later. These laws also protect the tattoo and body piercing practitioners from lawsuits by parents of minors who get body art. In some instances, parents have sued tattoo artists and piercing practitioners for tattooing or piercing their children without consent. In 2009, for example, a man sued a tattoo parlor in New Mexico for tattooing his daughter, who was under eighteen, without parental consent. The parlor's owner argued

Did You Know?

A tattoo starter kit that includes a tattoo machine and inks sells for ninety-nine dollars online.

that the girl showed identification that she was nineteen. He also stated that he did the work before the state's age limit and consent rules took effect.

As body art has become increasingly popular with teens, more states have enacted laws that require teens to get parental consent for both tattoos and piercings. In any state where tattoos are not prohibited for minors, they still must get parental consent to legally get a tattoo. An increasing number of states that allow minors to get pierced also require parental consent for piercings. For example, in July 2012 New York governor Andrew Cuomo signed a law that requires minors to obtain their parents' approval to get piercings other than on the earlobes. Cuomo explains the rationale for the law this way: "Body piercing can result in severe health risks and it is our obligation as New Yorkers and parents to make sure that our teens are taking every precaution to remain healthy and safe."[24] Parents must sign the consent in person at the time of the piercing. By August 2012 thirty-two states required some type of consent for a teen to get pierced.

There are two different types of consent—one is in-person consent, and the other is signed consent. In some states a teen who wants a tattoo or piercing must bring an adult with him or her to give the approval. For example, Virginia law requires a parent's presence when a minor gets a tattoo. Other states do not require the presence of an adult and instead only require teens to present a permission form signed by a parent or guardian. One such state is Florida, where teens aged sixteen through eighteen must give a notarized consent form signed by a parent or legal guardian to the tattoo studio.

Reaction to Consent Laws

In general, many parents approve of consent laws because their children are still minors and, they believe, need an adult's guidance when making decisions with long-lasting effects. Because tattoos and piercings can change their children's bodies forever and have health implications, parents contend they should be part of the decision-making process. Brenda Peterson of Lakeland, Florida, used that state's consent law to deny both her teenaged son and daughter permission to get tattoos as teens. Both got tattoos once they reached adulthood, but she does not regret that she

Laws differ from state to state on body piercings and tattoos for teens. Many states require parental consent under a certain age although some states prohibit certain types of body art for teens.

made them wait. "I figured it was an adult thing. I don't have a problem with tattoos in general, just not while underage,"[25] Peterson says.

Several piercing and tattoo studios implement their own policies regarding minors. They can require consent even if their studio is in a state that does not require consent. Owners of individual tattoo and piercing studios may choose to set age restrictions for their business as a precaution against lawsuits.

Prior to the New York law regarding consent for minors' piercings, Kingdom Tattoos, a tattoo and piercing studio in the West Village of New York, would not pierce anything other than earlobes for teens under eighteen unless a parent approved in person. Jennifer Herrera, a piercer at Kingdom Tattoos, said 50 percent of the people who came to her shop wanting piercings were under eighteen. She reported that they would come in, without parents, and beg for piercings. The youngest age of a hopeful customer was fifteen. But Herrera would not pierce this teen nor any others who were under eighteen because her shop required consent.

Some teens disagree with the parents, legislators, and business owners who support consent laws. These teens believe they are mature enough to make their own decisions about how to decorate their bodies. For some of these teens, if their parents do not give consent, they find alternate, illegal ways of getting pierced or tattooed.

Ignoring the Laws

Young people who are determined to get a piercing or tattoo usually manage to find a way around the laws. Most often they find someone who does tattoos or piercings without a license. These people are often found by word of mouth. Word also travels about licensed tattoo and piercing studios where the practitioners do not check IDs or consent forms. And occasionally teens choose to pierce or tattoo themselves or get a friend to do it.

Of all of the illegal methods, going to an unlicensed tattoo or piercing practitioner is the most common. The ability to learn techniques and order supplies online has contributed to a rise in the number of unlicensed practitioners. In the past, most tattoo equipment manufacturers would only sell the equipment to licensed artists who had learned the sanitary procedures that should accompany the tattoo process. Some manufacturers still only sell to licensed tattoo artists or studios, but these days just about anyone can go online and order a tattoo kit without providing proof of a license. Similarly, people can order piercing equipment online without attending any classes and instead learn to pierce through videos on the Internet. The result is that many people now have the equipment but not the professional training or knowledge to perform tattoos and piercings.

Tattoo parties, where teens obtain tattoos from unlicensed practitioners, have become popular in some states. For example, the Maine Center for Disease Control reported that the number of complaints regarding unlicensed tattoo artists rose from thirteen in 2010 to thirty-one in 2011. Several of the complaints were associated with tattoo parties,

Tattoo Parties

Tattoo parties are one way that teens greatly increase their risk of contracting a disease, developing an infection, or getting a poorly done tattoo. Tattoo parties are parties where teens and their friends tattoo one another or hire someone, typically unlicensed, to tattoo partygoers instead of going to a licensed tattoo parlor. Teens who choose to get tattoos at these parties typically do so because it is cheaper and no one usually asks about parental consent. In 2012 Kaitlin Chittenden of the Reston, Virginia, South Lakes High School received her first tattoo at a party and said, "When you get it done at a party it just means the cost of your tattoo will be significantly cheaper. It's definitely way more convenient for teenagers." The major problem is that those inking tattoos at parties often have not been trained in health and safety procedures or how to properly place and ink a tattoo. That is why they will ink the tattoos at rates much less than licensed practitioners.

Quoted in Olivia Hill, "Tattoo Parties Increase in Popularity Among Teens," *South Lakes High School Sentinel*, April 13, 2012.

get-togethers in private houses where an unlicensed tattoo artist inks minors who attend the parties. In Maine, anyone under eighteen may not legally get a tattoo, but such parties are one way teens are getting around the law.

Punishing Practitioners

Anyone who is caught illegally piercing or inking a minor may face fines and other punishment by the courts. Different states and cities impose different punishments. Some impose fines, others jail time, and others a combination of both.

In many states, parental consent laws no longer apply once a teen reaches eighteen. One young woman takes advantage of that type of law to get a piercing above her belly button.

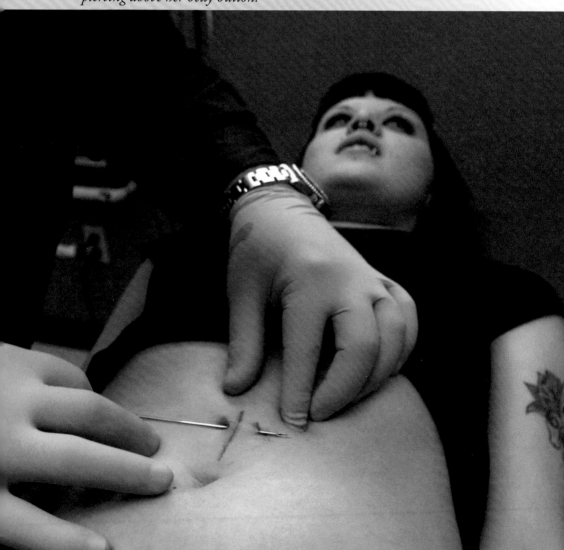

Brian Sporn discovered the penalty of tattooing a minor in Texas. Police in Texas received a tip that a fourteen-year-old had been tattooed at an unlicensed facility. Tattooing a minor is against the law in Texas regardless of consent. In 2012 police arrested Sporn and charged him with knowingly tattooing a minor and doing so in an unlicensed facility. Additionally, the fourteen-year-old's mother, Lydie Mathers, was arrested because she knowingly allowed her daughter to get tattooed despite Texas law. Both the tattooist and mother faced up to 180 days in prison.

Like tattooing, piercing minors also can result in jail time as Nicholas Gobert of Shreveport, Louisiana, discovered. He pierced the tongues of sixteen- and seventeen-year-old girls at Trendsetters Tattoo Shop in December 2011. Neither girl had written consent to receive piercings despite Louisiana law requiring such consent for anyone under eighteen. The owner of the shop and Gobert were arrested for the illegal piercing of minors and booked into Caddo Correctional Center.

Legal Repercussions for Teens

Teens also may face legal consequences if involved in illegal piercing or tattooing. For example, a teen can be charged with delinquency if he or she deliberately disobeys the law and gets pierced or tattooed without consent in states where consent is mandatory. Also, a teen can face legal trouble if he or she pierces or tattoos another teen.

In 2012 both a twelve- and fourteen-year-old suffered the consequences of illegal piercing. The parents of a twelve-year-old girl discovered that she had received a tongue piercing at a Delaware, Ohio, tattoo parlor, and the parents of a fourteen-year-old girl also discovered, a few days later, that their daughter's belly button had been pierced at the same studio. Neither girl had their parents' permission but was pierced anyway. Under Ohio law, piercings and tattoos may not be performed on those younger than eighteen without consent. The parents of both girls were livid at Jason Parks, the owner of the studio. Parks was charged with a count of contributing to the delinquency of a child, a first-degree misdemeanor. Juvenile courts also charged both of the girls with delinquency.

The mother of the twelve-year-old girl does not regret going to the police with her complaint even though it resulted in the charge against her daughter. "The girls were unruly," she said. "They did something they weren't supposed to do. . . . They have to pay the consequences for it."[26] In addition, the Delaware juvenile court system filed a count of unruliness, an unclassified misdemeanor, against each of the girls.

Another twelve-year-old girl also discovered the legal repercussions of piercing friends. In 2012 police arrested a girl from Georgia because she pierced another teen's navel at school. Georgia is a state that requires minors to obtain parent permission before piercing. A student from Moses Middle School came forward and let authorities know that the girl had pierced the navel of another student in the school's bathroom. The girl had watched a video on YouTube that taught how to pierce, then she bought the materials needed. The police charged the girl with piercing a minor and reckless conduct.

Parent or Guardian Involvement

Parents who break the laws regarding the tattooing and piercing of minors may also face legal punishment. Typically, these are cases involving parents who have, without a license, inked or pierced their child themselves or have taken their child to get inked or pierced even though such acts are illegal in that state.

Jerry Garrison of Jacksonville, Florida, discovered the implications of allowing a minor to get an illegal tattoo when he allowed his ten-year-old grandson, whom he had custody of, to get a tattoo. Florida law prohibits children under age sixteen to get tattooed unless it is for medical or dental reasons. Nevertheless, Garrison took his grandson to get a tattoo of the family initials on his right leg. The tattoo is a family tradition, the grandfather told NBC News.

Did You Know?

To be a licensed piercing artist in Oregon a person must meet several requirements, including proof of completion of an approved training program that entails 1,150 hours of combined theory and practical instruction and four hundred body piercing procedures.

Trend Reversal

While most states and cities have implemented stricter rules regarding minors and body art, Webster, a town in Massachusetts, has stepped in the other direction. In 2012 Webster's Board of Health voted 2-1 to allow minors aged fourteen to seventeen to get tattoos if they have written permission from a parent or guardian. Prior to this vote, those under eighteen could not get tattooed in Webster under any circumstances. The board's reasoning for the change is that reducing the age that teenagers can get legally tattooed will prevent them from getting unlicensed work.

When word of his actions reached the Florida Department of Children and Families, the agency removed the boy and other grandchildren from Garrison's care for various reasons including allowing the tattoo.

In a case in Georgia, Patty Marsh and her husband, Jacob Bartels, decided to tattoo their six children using a machine they made themselves out of a plastic pen and a needle made from guitar string that they connected to an electric motor. In 2010 both she and her husband were arrested for three counts each of illegal tattooing, second-degree child cruelty, and reckless conduct. Five of the children, whose ages ranged from ten to seventeen, got a cross tattoo on their hands and a sixth had "mom and dad" tattooed on his arm. Their parents had inked all of their tattoos and defended their actions by saying that their children wanted the tattoos and that they had a right, as parents, to tattoo their own children.

Odessa Clay also decided to tattoo her daughter, who was only eleven years old at the time. Clay has stated that her daughter asked for the tattoo, so she decided to comply, claiming she did not know it was illegal to tattoo anyone under the age of eighteen in North Carolina. Clay, who has several tattoos of her own, tattooed a heart shape on her daughter's shoulder in September 2012 and is now facing legal charges.

Consequences Matter

More parents, unlicensed tattooists and piercers, and teens may be arrested and face fines and potential jail time as regulations regarding minor body art become more stringent. Teens who try to get around the laws may find themselves not only in physical danger but also facing problems with the justice system. Teens who wish to get pierced or tattooed need to be aware of the laws that are in place and the implications of not following them.

Chapter Four

Pushing the Limits

A common reason that teens decide to get pierced and tattooed is to assert their individuality. However, as tattoos and piercings have become more popular, some teens have felt the need to go beyond the mainstream in decorating their bodies. In doing so, they have sometimes pushed the limits of what is socially acceptable and what their bodies can endure.

New Types of Piercings

In recent years some teens have taken to a new type of piercing called microdermals. Also known as single point piercings, this technique involves piercing the skin but instead of exiting the skin at another point in the usual way, a small anchor holds the piercing in place inside the skin. Protruding from the skin is the step, a post with a threaded hole that jewelry can be screwed into. The jewelry is interchangeable, as different pieces can be screwed into the step of the anchor. Unlike standard piercings, if a teen becomes tired of the microdermal, he or she cannot take it out alone. Instead, a piercer must use tools to remove it.

Another piercing variation is known as a surface piercing. With this technique, the piercing needle enters the skin in one spot, travels under the skin, and then comes out of the skin in another spot. Unlike a standard piercing, a surface piercing does not penetrate the skin deeply. Instead it travels a short distance right below the skin's surface. One attraction of this technique is that it allows a person to have piercings on parts of the body where standard piercing is not possible, such as the wrist. "I specifically got my surface piercing done because it is unique and different," says Betsy DeHaan. "I was the first person in my high school to have their nose pierced, but then a lot of people decided to get them as well. I then decided to pierce my wrist because I wanted to be more original and unique."[27]

Several complications can result from this process, including migration, a piercing that moves from its original location; rejection, a piercing that is pushed out of the skin; and damage to the skin tissue. Of all piercings, surface piercings have the highest rate of rejection. Many of these piercings migrate to the surface of the skin, then are pushed out and leave a permanent scar. Elayne Angel, a master piercer, writes that healing is notoriously difficult with these types of piercings and that scarring is more likely than with other forms of piercing.

Tattoos Beyond the Norm

Teens who want to do something a little different with tattoos have also looked for alternatives to the more standard inkings. Most people who get tattoos have them done in locations that can be covered by clothing. According to the Pew Research Center, 76 percent of women's tattoos and 68 percent of men's tattoos can be hidden by clothing. To be different, some teens have opted for larger, more visible tattoos that cannot be covered. These teens are placing tattoos in highly visible places, such as the hands and wrists, or they are getting bigger tattoos, such as full sleeve tattoos that cover most of the arm like a shirtsleeve.

Another way that teens have pushed the limits is to get multiple tattoos. For example, by her senior year in high school Alicia Young already had five tattoos on her body. "Since it is so much of a trend, people are getting a little bit excessive and outrageous,"[28] she says, explaining why she has multiple tattoos.

Famous teens are also turning to larger, more visible, and multiple tattoos. Kailyn Lowry, one of the teenage moms on MTV's reality show *Teen Mom 2*, not only has multiple tattoos but also extremely large ones. In 2012 she tweeted that a tattoo covering most of her back with the words "To the world you are one person, but to one person you are the world" was almost complete after seven sessions.

A Different Take on Tattoos

A more extreme way to imprint pictures and words on the body is a variation of tattooing known as scarification. Scarification involves scratching, etching, or cutting designs, pictures, or words into the skin and then allowing the scars to form the permanent design. Typically, during the scarification process a tattoo artist uses sterilized tools to cut patterns on the skin and then applies a substance such as hydrogen peroxide to irritate the cuts. Once scabs form and then peel away, a visible etching is left behind.

Jesse Villemaire, a licensed tattoo artist and piercer in Canada, performs scarification in addition to tattooing. Most of his clients who choose scarification are between the ages of eighteen and thirty-five. He consults with them before the scarification to make sure they understand the procedure and also that he cannot guarantee what the scar will look like once it is done. "It's impossible to tell someone how his or her scar will look once it's healed. Some people's scars will raise, some will indent, some will be very pink/red/purple while some people's will scar more white and hard,"[29] he explains.

Implanting a Bagel?

In 2012 a newer form of body modification became popular in Japan among its youth. Young adults decided to have saline solution injected into their foreheads to produce bagel shapes that protrude outward. To form a bagel-shaped forehead, a practitioner shoots saline into a person's forehead, which causes the forehead to swell. Once the saline has reached the point of puffiness, the practitioner makes it look like a bagel by pushing a thumb into the middle of the forehead. This makes an indent that is the center of the "bagel." Although unique, the imprint is not permanent, as the saline is absorbed into the body within sixteen to twenty-four hours.

Scarification (pictured) is a more extreme form of body art. It involves etching or cutting designs in the skin and allowing the scars to form a permanent design.

Another extreme variation of tattooing is branding, a process by which designs are burned onto the body. The procedure includes making a third degree burn on the skin that leaves a scar. The burn is made using a metal design shaped in words or pictures that the person has chosen to imprint on his or her skin. There are two main methods of making a third degree burn during this process. The first is to heat metal pieces that are cut into a design and then laid onto the skin. The other method is to use a thermo cautery unit, a machine typically used to stop bleeding by cauterization during surgery. This machine heats to 2000°F and leaves an immediate third degree burn on the skin. Body artists warn that having anyone other than a professional do this brand can lead to major burns and excessive scarring.

For decades, primarily African American college fraternities have used branding as part of their traditions. The branding is either done by a professional brander or by a fellow fraternity brother who is known as the "hit man." Some fraternities even have branding parties where more than one person is branded at the same time. In 2007 Kenny Curtis was branded as a member of Alpha Phi Alpha at the University of Wisconsin–Milwaukee and has favorable thoughts of his experience. "My family thought I was crazy for getting branded, but they all knew that I loved to be different,"[30] Curtis says.

A member of a different fraternity, Kappa Sigma, at Texas Christian Academy also experienced branding, but his experience was not positive. In 2010 Amon G. "Chance" Carter IV, at the time twenty years old, suffered second and third degree burns when fraternity members branded the group's Greek letters on his bottom with a hot coat hanger. This occurred during a party where Chance and others drank alcohol. The

Did You Know?

A corset piercing is made up of multiple surface piercings on the back arranged to look like a corset being laced up the body.

49

next day he awoke to much pain and eventually required surgery to correct the botched branding.

Both scarification and branding are much less common than tattoos because they are more dangerous. Each can lead to infections and other types of skin issues such as excessive scarring. Also, both can result in designs that do not look like what the person expected because the way a person's skin scars is unpredictable. Like most extreme body modifications, these types of body art can come with a price.

Adding to the Body

Subdermal implants, another form of extreme body art, appeal to some despite the risks. Subdermal implants are jewelry. They are placed completely under the skin so that, when healed, the jewelry itself cannot be seen but the raised designs of the piece are visible on the skin.

The Eyes Have It

One of the most extreme forms of tattooing is done on the whites of the eyes. This is extremely rare, but there are those who partake in this body modification. The process, known as scleral tattooing, uses the traditional method to tattoo the eye. Because the tattoo machine needle repeatedly pokes the eye, this process comes with extreme risks, including blindness. Despite the risks, there are those who want decorated eye whites and undergo the process. "It's amazing to me how different my eyes look from day to day because of the way the ink moves around, and also on how slowly the entire eye has become more and more blue," Shannon Larratt writes of her eye tattoos. She went on to write, "This modification has a good shot in the running to be my favorite modification of all time, both on myself and on others."

Shannon Larratt, "Blue Eyes Update," BME.com, December 14, 2012. http://news.bme.com.

The jewelry is implanted through a process called pocketing. During the pocketing process, the practitioner makes an incision in the skin's subcutaneous layer, which is under both the surface and epidermis layers of the skin. The incision is made with a subcutaneous elevator, an instrument developed specifically for this purpose. Next, the practitioner places the implant in a pocket between the skin layers. Lastly, the skin is stitched shut and the design, but not the actual implant, can be seen on the surface of the skin. These designs often are of stars, ridges, or barbells.

In 2010 twenty-one-year-old tattooed and pierced Evan discussed his implant on the *Dr. Phil* show, which features Phil McGraw, a celebrity psychologist. Evan showed off the inch-wide barbell implant that his friend had placed under the skin on the top of his hand years earlier. He explained that he chose to get an implant because he liked the looks of them.

Evan is lucky that he did not develop any health issues from the procedure because several risks are associated with this process, especially if it is not done by a professional. This is because the procedures involve opening the skin. Among the biggest risks are infection and scarring.

Stretching the Body

Rather than adding a design or implant to their body, some teens and young adults are drawn to physically altering the shape of their bodies. One process is stretching, or gauging. During this process a body part is stretched beyond its normal size. The most popular body part to stretch is the earlobe.

The first step in this process is to pierce the earlobe and then insert a small, cylindrical plug. Practitioners use plugs and other jewelry made from surgical stainless steel because this type of material does not absorb bacteria or dirt that can cause infections. The weight of surgical steel also helps the stretching process. That first implant is worn for about six weeks before it is removed and replaced with a slightly larger one. This one is left in the earlobe for four to eight weeks, depending on how quickly a person's earlobes heal. This may be done several times over the course of several months until the hole has stretched to the desired size. Body piercers say it is important to slowly increase the size of the earring to minimize the possibility of developing scar tissue. Once the earlobe is stretched to the desired size and healing is complete with no sign of infection, the temporary plug can be replaced with one made from wood or plastic or some other material.

Some of those who decide to stretch their earlobes do so as a way to rebel, but others just like the way it looks. Andrew B. says his decision to stretch his earlobes was not about nonconformity or rebellion. "I saw a guy with [stretched earlobes] at a pizza shop and thought it was pretty cool,"[31] he says.

Like most body art, stretching comes with health risks. These risks are more likely if a person tries to stretch the skin too quickly. One risk is blowouts—when a section of skin pushes out from inside the channel through the skin made by the piercing. Excessive scarring, also known as keloids, can also develop from this procedure. Teens who have the procedure done and then change their minds sometimes encounter problems such as the earlobes not completely closing or significant scarring.

Cutting the Body

An edgier way to change the body is to actually sculpt body parts, via cutting, to change how they look. In some cases these types of body modifications are illegal, and in all cases there are associated health risks. Despite these issues, some teens choose to go to these extremes to be different.

In the past decade certain people have been drawn to the look of elf ears, ears that look like those of fictional elves. To get these types of ears, people must have their ears sculpted. The process to achieve this look includes a practitioner slicing the top cartilage of the ear then sewing it back into a point. Unless the practitioner is a doctor, he or she cannot use anesthesia and the process is painful.

Serious teen and young adult fans of science fiction and fantasy, including movies such as *Avatar* and *Lord of the Rings*, are among those who have chosen to undergo the elf-ear procedure. "It was just something I thought would be fascinating," says Jordan Houtz, a young adult who underwent surgery for her elf ears. "I wouldn't go as far as saying Trekie, but definitely Lord of the Rings—all the sci-fi kind of stuff. It just fits my personality."[32]

The risks of this procedure are many, including the fact that the results are irreversible without plastic surgery. "This is one of those body mods where there's no turning back and where you need to find someone who knows what they're doing if you truly decide that such a modification is appropriate for you and your lifestyle,"[33] writes Rae Schwarz, body art editor of Bella Online. Additionally, doctors warn that those who undergo the procedure risk deformity of the ears and infection.

Split Tongues

Ears are not the only body part that people have chosen to cut in order to change their appearance. Another extreme body modification includes cutting the tongue from the tip to as far back as the underside base. The official name of this process is tongue bifurcation, but the more common name is splitting or forking the tongue.

There are three main methods used to fork a tongue, and all of these methods are painful. The first involves cutting the tongue down the middle with a scalpel and then stitching or suturing each half of the split tongue. The second method involves cauterization. With this method a cautery unit or an argon laser is used to burn the tongue in half. Last is the fishing method, when a person performs the tongue split himself or herself by using a fishing line to tie through an existing tongue piercing to the tip of the tongue. The line is then tightened to the point where it cinches through the tissue and cuts through the tongue over a week or two.

The person who developed the fishing line approach is a certified body piercer who wanted to try something new. At nineteen years old, professional body piercer Dustin Allor decided to split her tongue on her own and developed the fishing method. Allor explains that the reason she did this and other extreme types of body modification is that she believes they are beautiful ways of changing her body. "I have differing views from the majority on what beauty is. I don't think of my body as just a canvas anymore, it is a piece of clay that can be molded and sculpted,"[34] she says.

Anyone choosing to split his or her tongue may suffer major drawbacks. Tongue splitting can cause speech problems after the process is completed and major blood loss during the process. Another drawback

Some young people have chosen to alter the appearance of their ears or tongue. The process of tongue bifurcation, also known as splitting or forking the tongue, is painful no matter what method is used.

is that a person can get in legal trouble for splitting the tongue, as it is illegal in some states such as Illinois.

On the Extremes

New ways to change and add to the body are constantly being developed as people seek to achieve nonconformity. As long as teens search for ways to display their uniqueness to others, they will likely delve into extreme body modifications. However, these teens may be putting themselves at significant health risks and suffer drawbacks later in life due to these decisions.

Did You Know?
Illinois, New York, Delaware, and Texas all have laws that ban or limit tongue bifurcation.

Chapter Five

Body Art Regrets

As years pass, people's bodies, emotions, and life situations change. These types of changes can lead to changes in people's feelings about their body art. Many people who got pierced or tattooed as teens remain happy with their decisions, but others come to regret their choices. Their reasons for unhappiness vary, but many say they were too young when they got their body art. For those who wish to rid themselves of their body art, there are options, but not all are totally effective.

Rising Regrets

Statistics show that many people wish they could reverse body art decisions made when they were young. A 2012 online Harris Poll found that while 86 percent of people with tattoos do not regret getting them, 14 percent do. Another study by Mayo Clinic found that nearly half of college students who get tongue piercings decide to let them close after college.

Studies in other countries have found the rising number of people getting tattoos and piercings has resulted in increasing regrets. A 2012 study in Great Britain sought to find out how often people with visible tattoos regret getting them. The six-month study surveyed people with visible tattoos who visited the dermatology department of East Lancashire Hospitals. The study found that nearly one-third of survey participants regretted their tattoos. Men who got their tattoos before the age of sixteen were three times more likely to regret their tattoos than other survey participants. Also, people with tattoos on the upper part of the body more often regretted their tattoos than those with tattoos on lower body parts.

Dermatologists and plastic surgeons say they are seeing an increase in patients who want to rid themselves of their body art. For example, a California chain of tattoo laser removal stores, called Dr. Tattoff, has seen business boom since opening in 2004. The stores have seen more than thirteen thousand clients with the majority being women aged twenty-five to thirty-five, says James Morel, the company's chief executive officer.

Too Soon

One reason that people say they regret their body art is that they got their body art at too young an age. For example, Cassandra Martins got her first and only tattoo at age fifteen with the consent of her mother. A few years later, when she entered college, she already regretted her choice and underwent laser tattoo removal. "Nobody under 18 knows what he or she wants forever. I cringe when I hear young people talk about inking themselves. I don't (think) the concept of 'permanent' or 'forever' resonates well with the young,"[35] Martins says. The Harris Poll found the number one reason people say they regret their tattoo is that they were too young when they got it.

Celebrities who chose to ink while young also are among those who end up regretting their early choices. Pop star Demi Lovato admits that she wishes she had been more thoughtful when she chose to get twelve tattoos as a teen. In 2012, at age twenty, Lovato talked about how she has considered removing some of her tattoos. In an interview she pointed to a drawing of her friend's lips on the inside of her left forearm, and called the tattoo "a spur of the moment, stupid decision."[36]

Like tattoos, piercing can also result in regrets. Michelle Robertson thought that at eighteen she was capable of well thought out, adult decisions and decided to get a navel piercing. She admits that she ignored warnings about the health risks and got one soon after turning eighteen without thinking about potential problems. "The piercing signified my acceptance into adulthood. It was my defining act of parental defiance, and I relished not having to ask my mom to sign the waiver to get the piercing," Robertson writes. "Three days later, when the open wound in my midsection began oozing a sticky yellow liquid, I no longer felt like the mature, independent adult in the tattoo shop earlier that week."[37] Six months later the infection had healed and the piercing closed. Robertson was happy to return to being un-pierced.

Displeased with the Look

Regrets about body art choices made when a person was young can also stem from how the tattoo turned out. Sometimes the tattoo artist is not able to ink the design exactly like the picture the person chose or designed. Also, the tattoo may stretch or fade over time. Some fading typically occurs a year after the tattoo is completed. More extensive fading is likely if the tattoo is on a body part that is exposed to the sun. As for stretching, a tattoo stretches if a person's body changes from weight gain or weight loss. Lastly, the tattooist may not ink the tattoo in the exact place the person envisioned. For example, Kailyn Lowry's body is decorated with numerous tattoos, but she came to regret one of them because of its location. A tattooist inked "Pride Over Pity" on her shoulder, but Lowry was not happy with its positioning. She became so regretful that she decided to start the laser tattoo removal process. "Think hard before you ink!" Lowry tweeted in July 2012. "Just finished my second laser tattoo removal treatment."[38]

There are also cases of tattooists who make mistakes when working on a client. In 2012 Jerri Peterson proudly carried the Olympic torch as part of the 2012 Olympic torch relay. To commemorate this special event in her life, Peterson decided to get the Olympic rings and the words "Olympic Torch Bearer" tattooed on her arm. After the tattoo artist completed the work, she discovered Olympic had been spelled "Oylmpic" and was left with a permanent misspelling on her body.

Those who get pierced may also end up unhappy with the result, or their bodies may not accept the piercing. As can happen with tattoos, the practitioner may not place the piercing in the

> ## Did You Know?
> Employment is the most common reason given for tattoo removal; 40 percent of respondents cited this reason in a survey published in 2012 by the Patient's Guide.

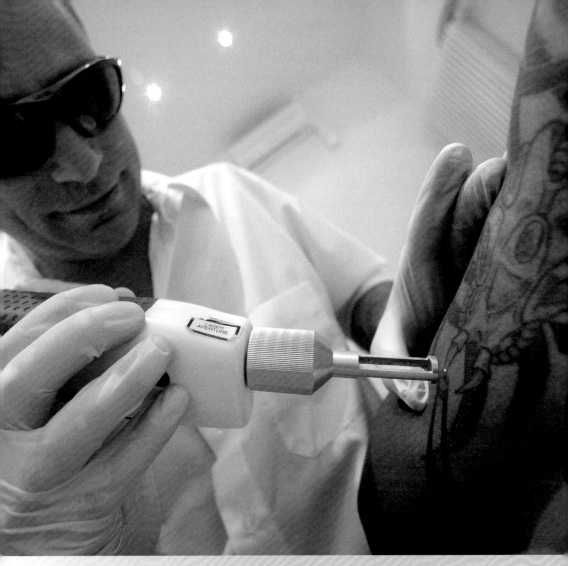

A technician uses a laser device to remove a tattoo. Informal surveys suggest that tattoo regrets are most common in people who obtained tattoos in their youth.

exact place the person envisioned. Also, the piercing itself can change on its own, and a person's body may reject it. Over time, a piercing can migrate, or move from its original spot closer to the surface of the skin, and eventually push itself out of the body. "I have had all three of my rejected piercings migrate after they were four years old. That seems to be a limit that my body has determined for foreign objects and after that length of time it says, 'Time to go!'"[39] writes Karen Hudson.

Different Stage in Life

People go through different stages of life, and new stages can result in a desire to rid themselves of old piercings or tattoos. For example, a person may get several piercings as a rebellious teen but then ends up as a college graduate who desires a professional job and is hindered by his or her body art.

Plastic surgeons, dermatologists, and tattoo removal specialists often see college graduates coming in to remove or cover up their body art. Plastic surgeon D.J. Verret repairs a variety of body art issues and has found that many of his patients are those who are looking to start their careers. "The biggest age group coming for repair," says Verret, "are high school and college graduates entering the job market."[40]

Kaylie (a pseudonym) is among those who found that body art can be a hindrance when starting a career. Kaylie got a tattoo on the upper part of her chest while on a beach trip celebrating high school graduation. She and three friends were tattooed with matching iguanas to

Starred for Life

Imagine regretting not one, not two, but fifty-six tattoos. Every morning when she looks in a mirror Kimberley Vlaeminck regrets her fifty-six tattoos. In 2009 eighteen-year-old Vlaeminck opted to get fifty-six stars tattooed on her face. Soon after, she claimed she only asked for three stars then fell asleep as the tattoo artist placed more on her face. Later, she renounced this claim, saying she had lied because she did not want her parents to know she willingly was tattooed with fifty-six stars. She regrets getting the tattoos and wants them off but, as of 2012, the tattoos were still there. In order to remove them, she needs approximately $18,000, and professionals have said that even after the laser removal process, remnants of the stars would likely still be visible.

symbolize their friendship. After college Kaylie opted to remove her tattoo to improve her job prospects. "I was tired of wearing turtle necks to job interviews, and I didn't like the way the more closed-minded people judged me just because I had a tattoo,"[41] she says. She spent more than $2,000 on laser treatments to remove the tattoo and is among many who are willing to part with their money to rid themselves of old body art.

Tattoo Removal

Removing body art, particularly tattoos, is not an easy or inexpensive process. Despite these drawbacks, the tattoo removal business has grown significantly in recent years. A study conducted by the Patient's Guide, a website dedicated to providing information about medical issues, found that the number of tattoo removal procedures in North American doctors' offices grew by 32 percent from 2011 to 2012.

Several tattoo removal methods are available, including surgical excision, dermabrasion, and laser removal. All of these processes come with risks and can be quite expensive. Burns, scars, and other health issues also can result from any of these processes. Lastly, none of the processes are 100 percent effective.

Surgical incision and dermabrasion are less commonly used removal methods due to their side effects. With surgical incision, the patient's tattooed skin is cut out with a scalpel, and the wound is closed with stitches. This almost always results in a scar; a large tattoo removed this way can leave a large scar. Dermabrasion is "sanding" the skin—removing the surface and middle layers of the tattoo with a high-speed rotary device that has an abrasive wheel or brush. The tattooed area of skin is anesthetized during the process, and often the patient is also given a sedative to help him or her remain calm. This process leaves the sanded skin raw and sore for over a week until it heals. Even if the skin heals properly, scarring is possible.

Today, the most popular method of tattoo removal is with a laser. Laser removal does a better job of removing the tattoo than the other methods, and it does so with the fewest side effects. During this process the dermatologist points a high-intensity laser beam at the tattooed design. Specifically, dermatologists use instruments called Q-switched lasers on the tattoo to heat and break the tattoo pigments into particles that are absorbed by the body. According to Suzanne Kilmer, a dermatologist and laser researcher in Sacramento, California, the full removal of a tattoo takes an average of eight treatments, spaced at least a month apart, using different wavelengths of the Q-switched lasers (QSL) for each ink color.

Tattoo Removal Difficulties

Though laser removal is more effective than the other methods, it is not always 100 percent successful. Whereas some tattoos are relatively simple to remove, others are more difficult for reasons that may include size and color. Even with laser removal, some remnants of the tattoo may remain.

The factors that make laser tattoo removal more difficult were studied by the American Medical Association (AMA) and summarized in a 2012 report. The study was conducted at a laser surgery center in Milan, Italy, from 1995 through 2010 and included 352 people, of which 201 were men, and the median age was thirty years. The study discovered what factors made laser removal less effective.

Tattoo ink color had a major effect on removal success. During the study, 47 percent of the people had their tattoos successfully removed after ten laser treatments. Of these, researchers found that tattoos with mainly black and red pigments were the most easily removed, but other colors were more difficult. For example, 58 percent of all black tattoos were removed with ten sessions and 51 percent of tattoos with just red and black ink were removed in the same number of sessions. Researchers found that the black and red inks absorb the wavelength light emitted by the QSL better than other colors. Greens, yellows, or blues in a tattoo reduce removal chances by as much as 80 percent.

Temporary Options

One way to avoid any issues with removing permanent body art is to not get permanent body art in the first place. Temporary body art is an option that allows a teen to experiment with different looks without risking regret. For someone who wants a tattoo, temporary tattoos can be painted, airbrushed, drawn, or transferred to the skin through paper, ink, and glue. Also available are henna tattoos, known as Mehndi; using a paste made from the powdered leaves of the henna plant to draw delicate designs on the skin. For those who want tongue or other types of piercings, magnetic piercings are an option as is clip-on jewelry. These options can allow a teen to try different body art without making a lifelong commitment.

The study also found that tattoo removal success is less likely to succeed if the person is a smoker, if the design is larger than twelve inches, or if the tattoo is older than thirty-six months. The reason smoking is thought to make removal more difficult is that smoking is known for preventing wounds from healing quickly. Large tattoos are more difficult to remove for the simple fact that it takes longer to remove greater amounts of ink. Older tattoos are more difficult to remove since the ink has moved deeper into the skin.

Barriers to Removal

Certain barriers prevent some people who want to remove their tattoos from doing so. One barrier to tattoo removal is pain. Stephanie Gorchynski had two black-ink death angels, also known as grim reapers, tattooed onto her back, and by her thirties she regretted both of them. She opted to undergo laser removal and said the pain was excruciating and gave her blisters all over the area where her tattoos were removed. Such pain discourages others from getting their tattoos removed.

A New York woman displays the remains of a spider tattoo she tried to have removed. Some tattoos can be removed with relative ease but others can never be completely erased.

Cost is another barrier to many who want their tattoos removed. Gorchynski spent thousands of dollars to remove her tattoos, but many others cannot afford to do so. Getting a tattoo may have cost a person relatively little, such as a couple of hundred dollars, in comparison to removal costs that could run into the thousands. At Dr. Tattoff tattoo removal studios in California, removal costs thirty-nine dollars per square inch of tattoo for each treatment. Most tattoos are more than just one square inch and typically take an average of eight sessions to remove.

Tattoo Removal Programs

Former gang members who want to leave their old lives behind often seek to rid themselves of gang-related tattoos that visually tie them to their old gangs. Programs that pay for their tattoo removals are available to help these former gang members.

Homeboy Industries, based in California, is one of the charities that provides free tattoo removal to former gang members who want to start new lives. This organization helps approximately twelve thousand former gang members remove their tattoos each year. Troy, a volunteer doctor with the organization, says the organization targets tattoos that prevent the former gang members from getting jobs. "We focus on the visible ones," says Troy, "the ones that make you a target when you're walking decades later with your son and somebody shoots you, or the ones that prevent you from getting a job."[42]

Piercing Removal Problems

Piercing removal is not as intense or expensive as tattoo removal, but like tattoo removal, it may not be entirely successful. For most piercings the removal is fairly simple, but the results vary. These results may require intervention by a dermatologist or other health professional.

In most cases, the process used to remove a piercing is straightforward. Elayne, professional piercer, says that people can remove their piercing only if it is in good health, meaning without infection. If the piercing is in good health, she says, the wearer should wash his or her hands and just remove the jewelry. Then, let the hole close on its own.

One complication is that not all holes will close—whether they do or not depends on the piercing's size and placement. In the case of a hole that does not completely close, a plastic surgeon may need to close it surgically. Another issue is that major scars, such as keloids, can develop even if the piercing closes. Although

Did You Know?

A piercing that is abandoned but does not close up may excrete sebum, a combination of fat and cellular material from the body.

rare, at times keloids reach the point that they need to be surgically removed. Lastly, another potential issue with removal is that if piercing jewelry is removed while the piercing is infected, the infection can worsen and require treatment. Piercings, like other body art, can leave long-lasting issues even after removal.

Long-Term Implications

Because of the issues associated with reversing permanent body art, body art professionals highly recommend people take time when making a decision to get a tattoo, piercing, or other type of permanent decoration. Teens in particular need to consider the long-term implications of body art because of the changes that will eventually occur in their lives. Making a quick decision regarding body art as a teen could result in great cost, both monetarily and emotionally, later in life.

Introduction: More than a Trend

1. Quoted in Ann Oldenburg, "One Direction's Harry Styles Gets New Chest Tattoo," *Delaware Online*, November 9, 2012. www.delaware online.com.

2. Flutter, "Why I Love My Tattoo," January 22, 2012. http://flutter brush.wordpress.com.

3. Quoted in L. Lopez, "Students Stand Out Through Their Body Art," *North Hardin News*, September 2012. http://nhhsnews.com.

Chapter One: Adorning Their Bodies

4. Quoted in Markus Cuff, "Kimberly O'Connor," *Tattoo*, August 2012, p. 9.

5. Quoted in Meagan McDougall, "Young People Addicted to Ink," *Concordian*, March 9, 2012. http://theconcordian.org.

6. Glenn Braunstein, "Drilling Down on Body Piercing Health Issues," *Huffington Post*, May 21, 2012. www.huffingtonpost.com.

7. Quoted in McDougall, "Young People Addicted to Ink."

8. Quoted in Stacey Goldmeier, "Tattoo Influence and Teens," Ezine .com, August 25, 2010. http://EzineArticles.com.

9. Quoted in Ann Rappoport, "Tattoo or Not To and Other Piercing Questions," MetroKids, January 2012. www.metrokids.com.

10. Quoted in "13-Year-Old Cancer Survivor Talks About Illegal Tattoo," KIRO TV, August 8, 2012. www.kirotv.com.

11. Quoted in Goldmeier, "Tattoo Influence and Teens."

12. Quoted in Briana Tomlinson, "Teens and Tattoos: 'Think Before You Ink,'" *Huffington Post*, February 27, 2012. www.huffington post.com.

13. Amy Kaufman, "I Tried to Hide My Tattoo from My Parents," Gurl.com, July 3, 2012. www.gurl.com.

Chapter Two: Body Art Risks

14. Michelle Silverthorne, "My Turn: What Happens After Hepatitis," *Newsweek.com*, January 10, 2010. www.thedailybeast.com.

15. Quoted in Scott Hensley, "Tattoo Ink Linked to Serious Skin Infections," NPR.org, August 23, 2012. www.npr.org.

16. Quoted in Meghan Kalkstein, "Teen's Mom: My Son Ended Up in the ER After Getting Tattoos," KATU News, October 13, 2012. www.katu.com.

17. Quoted in Sam Kennedy, "Tattooed Job-Seekers May Have Tough Time Getting Hired," *Inquirer*, May 29, 2012. www.philly.com.

18. Quoted in Andrew Moran, "Catholic School Student Kicked Out of Class Over Lip Piercing," *Examiner*, February 3, 2011. www.examiner.com.

19. Quoted in *PreMedLife*, "Book Excerpt: The Medical School Admissions Guide: A Harvard MD's Week-by-Week Admissions Handbook," August 15, 2012. www.premedlife.com.

20. Quoted in Christi Lowe, "Teen's Tattoo Leads to Criminal Charges," December 15, 2008. www.wral.com.

Chapter Three: Body Art, Teens, and the Law

21. Quoted in Beth Whitehouse, "Parental Guidance: No Tattoos for Minors," Exploreli.com, July 5, 2011. http://long-island.newsday.com.

22. Quoted in ThreeSixty, "It's the Law: No More Tattoos for Minors," September 24, 2010. www.threesixtyjournalism.org.

23. Quoted in ThreeSixty, "It's the Law: No More Tattoos for Minors."

24. Quoted in James Arkin, "Cuomo: Law Protects Teens from Piercing Risks," *New York Daily News*, July 30, 2012. www.nydailynews.com.

25. Quoted in Anne-Louise Munroe, "Teens and Tattoos: Some Parents Grant Permission, Others Make Kids Wait," *Lakeland (FL) Ledger*, October 3, 2010. www.theledger.com.

26. Quoted in Quan Truong and Allison Manning, "Moms React Sharply to Girls' Illicit Piercings," *Columbus Dispatch*, February 4, 2012. www.dispatch.com.

Chapter Four: Pushing the Limits

27. Quoted in Sarah States, "Modifying Bodies," *Chimes*, November 16, 2007. http://clubs.calvin.edu.

28. Quoted in Briana Tomlinson, "Teens and Tattoos."

29. Quoted in Thrive Studios, "Scarification Interview," 2012. www.thrivestudios.ca.

30. Quoted in Ashley Battle, "For Some Black Fraternities, Body Branding Is a Symbol of Devotion," *Columbia News Service*, March 27, 2007. http://jscms.jrn.columbia.edu.

31. Quoted in Mary Fetzer, "Teen Piercing Trends: Earlobe Gauging, Stretching and Body Piercing," She Knows, April 22, 2011. www.sheknows.com.

32. Quoted in Andrea Canning, "Elf Ears Are the Rage Among Quirky Young Adults," ABC News, April 7, 2012. http://abcnews.go.com.

33. Rae Schwarz, "Are Elf Ears the Next Must Have Body Art?," Bella Online, 2012. http://www.bellaonline.com.

34. Dustin Allor, "Modified Nut," 2005. http://dustin2dust.com.

Chapter Five: Body Art Regrets

35. Quoted in Sarah LeTrent, "Tattoos and Piercings: How Young Is Too Young?," CNN, July 12, 2012. www.cnn.com.

36. Quoted in Zach Johnson, "Demi Lovato Regrets Getting 12 Tattoos Before Age 20," *US Magazine*, September 8, 2012. www.usmagazine.com.

37. Michelle Robertson, "Piercing the Way to Maturity," *Daily Californian*, August 20, 2012. www.dailycal.org.

38. Quoted in Mehera Bonne, "Kailyn Lowry Undergoes More Laser Treatment for Tattoo Removal!," *Wet Paint*, July 18, 2012. www.wetpaint.com.

39. Karen Hudson, "Body Piercing Rejection and Migration," About.com, 2012. http://tattoo.about.com.

40. Quoted in Mary Fetzer, "Teen Piercing Trends."

41. Quoted in Fox Business, "Ink Regret: Job Seekers Seek Tattoo Removal to Increase Job Prospects," May 23, 2012. www.foxbusiness.com.

42. Quoted in *Economist*, "Where Homies Can Heal," February 18, 2012. www.economist.com.

For Further Research

Books

Elayne Angel, *The Piercing Guide to Aftercare and Troubleshooting*. New York: Random House, 2013.

Genia Gaffaney, *The Art of Body Piercing: Everything You Need to Know Before, During, and After Getting Pierced*. Bloomington, IN: iUniverse, 2013.

Gregory Hall, *Tattoos: Should I or Shouldn't I?* Cleveland, OH: Gregory Hall, MD, 2011.

Pete Peterson, *Tattoo Removal: The Modern Guide to Tattoo Removal and Fading*. Seattle: Amazon Digital Services, 2012.

Frank Spalding, *Erasing the Ink: Getting Rid of Your Tattoo*. New York: Rosen, 2011.

Websites

Alliance of Professional Tattooists (www.safe-tattoos.com). This website provides information about the tattoo business.

Association of Professional Piercers (www.safepiercing.com). This website provides information about safe piercing practices and current piercing legislation.

Centers for Disease Control and Prevention (www.cdc.gov). This website provides health information for the United States and has specific articles regarding tattoos, body piercing, and their related health issues.

Mayo Clinic (www.mayoclinic.com). This website provides health information and includes various articles about the health implications of tattoos and body piercing.

Internet Sources

Steven Dowshen, "What Is a Body Piercing and What Can You Expect?," KidsHealth, February 2012. http://kidshealth.org/teen/your _body/body_art/body_piercing_safe.html. This article provides specific information about piercing procedures and precautions.

Nerino Petro, "Think Before You Tat—Can Body Art Affect Your Employment Opportunities?," Compujurist, September 2012. http://com pujurist.com/2010/01/22/think-before-you-tat-can-body-art-affect -your-employment-opportunities. This article discusses how tattoos can affect job possibilities.

Mary Pflum, "Teens and Tattoos: Would You Let Your Teen Get Inked?," ABC News, October 12, 2010. http://abcnews.go.com/GMA /Parenting/tattoos-teens-parents-teens-body-art/story?id=11849086# .ULaqxqn3CqQ. This article discusses parents' reactions and thoughts about teens and tattoos.

Magazines

Polly Gee, "My Best Friend and I Are Both Getting the Same Tattoo," *Tattoo*, August 2012. This article delves into the reasons behind tattoos.

Durb Morrison, "All in the Family," *Tattoo*, August 2012. This article provides information about Durb Morrison, tattoo artist.

Index

Cover: © Markus Cuff/Corbis, Thinkstock Images

AP Images: 9, 48, 54, 59, 64

Dr. P. Marazzi/Science Photo Library: 30

© Markus Cuff/Corbis: 19

Thinkstock Images: 15, 25, 37

Jose Luis Villegas/Zuma Press/Newscom: 40

Leanne Currie-McGhee lives in Norfolk, Virginia, with her daughters, Hope and Grace, and husband Keith. She has enjoyed writing educational books for over ten years.